Still I Stand

Still I Stand

poems

Roosevelt Richards

VILLAGE TALES PUBLISHING

ISBN: 9781945408083
LCCN: 2017930124
eISBN:9781945408090

Village Tales Publishing provides traditional publishing services and turnkey services to individuals that seek to successfully self-publish and promote their books. We handle all aspects of publishing—editing, cover design, production, marketing and order fulfillment.

Please visit our websites:
www.villagetalespublishing.com
www.oass.villagetalespublishing.com

Printed in the United States of America

Dedication

This book is dedicated to the greatest man that ever set foot upon this earth, Napoleon Francis Richards, my Daddy.

You made growing up so much fun Dad, you are a part of almost all my fondest memories and it is so sad that you couldn't see your lil man growing up to be who he is today. After everything you did, after all the sacrifices, after all the blood, tears and pain, you couldn't reap what you sowed. It's sad that you never got to see your grandson we always talked about.

You taught me to believe in myself and never quit no matter what, you taught me to go out and seize opportunity, and not wait for them. You taught me to be better today than what I was yesterday, you taught me to be the best version of myself, you taught me to put family over everything. You are a legend for me and our family, Dad. You will always be my hero. Thank you, Daddy... Live on.

This is for you.

Acknowledgement

I am extremely grateful to my mother, Rose White Richards, for all the motivation, advice and support during this project; for the constant reminders of, "Micki, are you not writing today?"

To my friend, Bernice Ruz Thomas, who patiently read through everything, including the garbage and told me how much she enjoyed reading and re-reading;

To my little brother, Dikena Jackson, who never ceased to have my back in everything I do, and who is always my first critic;

To my beloved son, Roosevelt Delvin Richards Jr., who gives me a reason every day to be a better person, even by the way he laughs or looks at me and his mother, Sonia Warth Jalloh, who no matter what, encourages me to pursue my dreams and let me know I can be better than who I am;

To my niece, Danielle Cutie Sowogie, for loving everything I do.

I am particularly indebted to Madam Ophelia S. Lewis for giving me hope when I was so discouraged about taking my work forward, for believing in me when no other publisher would even respond to my email, for the constant reminders when work clouded everything, and for the opportunity and encouragement. I will never forget the first feedback "Awesome poems, Roosevelt. Why have you stopped writing? How can I get to motivate you?"

Thank you!

Contents

Intricacies of Life

Life's full of many sorrows,
I wish I could predict tomorrow;
But determination is a way forward,
That can only be achieved through willpower.

Except in your quest to achieve success,
Life will forever be a long process;
And many hindrances you must overcome,
Never knowing what you will become.

But faith is something you can depend on,
And hope, you must lay your head upon;
For in these dark tunnels of twists and turns,
There will always be light at the end.

Random

The last rays of the sun is gone,
And nightfall has come again.
The day job is done,
And gallivanting begins.

Some go to witness movies,
Others stay to play games,
Some go and relax at the grooves,
Others stay to seek their dreams.

Some go to candlelight dinners,
Others stay and use their cells,
Some think of Jesus's Kingdom,
Others prefer thinking of hell.

When the sun rises in the east,
And the world comes alive again,
The night has been a feast,
But the day has just begun.
Others with better voice may pray,
And gain from the Cirrhaean city answer kind.

Seasons

The leaves are green
Like the apron of an old Dane;
Flying in the wind
When there is so much rain.

It swishes and swirls;
The wind makes it twirl
Amidst all the whirls,
It sounds like Daddy's rail.

Then the leaves fall,
But the trees remain standing tall;
It's as empty as a hall
When there is no wall.

The leaves are brown,
And one by one they come down;
But yet the world shines
Like the lilies of the rhine.

Expectations

Whenever
  You see electricity
    In a once noble candle city,
      Just remember,
        A female's generosity
          Have brought us such capacity.

Whenever
  You see dilapidated buildings
    Standing in the middle
      Of nowhere without a ceiling,
        Just remember,
          A male political standing
            Has caused us
              To look a little bit degrading.

Let Liberia Be Liberia Again

Let Liberia be Liberia again;
Let it be the dream it use to be,
Let it be one nation free from slain,
Let it be the home known for the free.

Let Liberia be the dream our ancestors dreamed;
Let it be Africa's first nation standing all alone,
Where dictators never succeeded,
Nor monarchy reign,
Until our good old Lord is ready to dethrone.

Let my land be a land where liberty is priceless;
And its citizens are free from prejudice,
Where opportunities are real,
And life is free and endless.

Let Liberia be Liberia again;
The land where every man is free,
The land that came through bullets,
Bloodshed and death,
Yet all the fields are green.

Where colonialism has left no stain,
But we the people are yet to redeem;
The mighty landscapes and our endless dreams,
And make Liberia, Liberia again.

Liberia

For fourteen wasted years,
My country has shared tears;
But it has always been in my prayers,
So don't ask, "Who cares?"

With bullets flying everywhere,
And babies dropping here and there;
My country, beautiful, yet so scared,
Crumbled, before my very stare.

Bloodshed, the order of the day,
Former wise men killing for pay;
Who then can posterity say,
"This man is a true patriot, come what may."

Little boys, strung high on drugs,
Shooting people down like grown thugs;
Can't even appreciate a mother's hug,
God, have we run out of luck?

Death

If death be so cruel,
Then only the wicked he should slay;
And think about the duel,
He'll encounter each day.

He cuts a promising life short,
As if he is the boss;
So many families stay in shock,
As if there is no God.

Some people live for just hours,
While others see a lifetime;
But death is such a coward,
Only the wicked he leaves unharmed.

I wonder, Master Jesus,
When I become a man;
I'll triumph like Julius Ceasar,
And thwart death's every plan.

Oh death, if you're so valiant,
Then the wicked you must slay;
Else's I will inherit my savior's talent,
And you won't see another day.

If There Be One Favor I May Ask

If there be one favor I may ask,
Let it be for the commemoration
Of those gallant men and women
Who pick up arms to defend their sovereignty;
Who stayed incarcerated
Because their people were not free,
Who disobeyed orders to save lives,
Who accepted insults,
Yet defended their positive causes,
Who sacrificed their lives
For people who didn't understand their motives.

Let it be for those who died
So others could live,
Who saw the light
And embraced it,
Who compromised their meager
 To enable others to carry on.

Let it be for those
Indiscriminate men and women
On ladder 29,
Who entered hell
So others could reach heaven,
Who aborted their lifelong dreams
So their people could succeed.

Who persevered
And remained dauntless in defeat,
Who withstood mockery and contempt
To protect our heritage,

Who expended their resources
For the development of mankind,
Who dreamed dreams
For racial, tribal and gender equalities.

Let it be for those men and women
Who fought so hard
For the accomplishments of today,
That was forever a dream
During their lifetime.

Like Lincoln,
King,
Mendela,
Obama,
Like my Daddy...

Forever Young

I wish I was forever young,
To roam the world far and wide;
I'll do everything to keep me strong
And find myself a Bride.

I would take up time for every sport
And learn it to my best;
I'll even learn how to row a boat
And pass my every test.

I would fly a plane
And live my dream;
For life is but a game
And only winners can win.

Our Knight

Last night I dreamed my Daddy
Came back to me on Friday;
A man so strong,
He died too young.

He lived a life
Adoring his wife,
He strived to succeed
Fulfilling our needs.

My Daddy was gallant,
A man so brilliant;
Only if the world knew
How Daddy would have been healed.

And as he grew old,
As the tale was told;
This man, so bold,
Incited many crowds
That today makes us proud.

My Daddy left a legacy,
His life will never be a fallacy;
But who can this legend be,
Just plain, old, simple me!

Mama

Once upon a memory,
I lied in an infirmary;
Someone wiped away my tears,
Someone who really cares... Mama.

When I was mad for nothing,
Or had a headache and fronting,
Someone always held me close,
Even though I had a running nose... Mama.

When I threw a tantrum,
And people called me, Wanton,
Someone protected me with a punishing smile,
I've always remembered,
Even if at a thousand miles... Mama.

When the coach said I wasn't good enough,
And I thought I'll just self-destruct;
Someone taught me never to quit,
And never in life to hate... Mama.

When I had my first heartbreak,
And the pain was so real, I couldn't take,
Someone taught me to be strong.
Believe in God and live long... Mama.

When I disobeyed and got into trouble,
And there was nothing around me, but rubbles,
Someone fished me out in the middle of the night,
And still believed her baby boy was bright... Mama.

If I've never said, "Thank you,"
For bringing me into this world,
I'd like to say that now;
"Thank you, Mama, for everything."

Wonderful God

As I sit at my window
    Watching the rolling hills,
I wonder how God can handle
    So much without a bill.

He gave the trees their greenery,
    And fully replenish their leaves;
He gave the world a scenery
    That only artist believes.

He gave the sun the power
    To brighten the world each day;
He also makes the flowers
    To blossom come every May.

He does many wonderful things,
    So many I cannot say;
Oh God, what a supreme being,
    I'll serve you every day.

I Wonder

I wonder how my life will be
    Five years from now;
I wonder who my friends will be
    If my life turns around.

I wonder how the world would have been
    If blacks were still legally slaves;
I wonder if Obama would have ran
    Had he been born in a cave.

I wonder if Rosa Park would have lived
    If she had been born in my days;
I wonder if her descendants are as brave
    As their grandmother was in those days.

I wonder if America would have succeeded,
    If those gallant men hadn't found land;
I wonder if July 4th would ever have been celebrated,
    If America had failed to stand.

I wonder where the Good Lord was,
    When Lucifer initiated his wicked plans;
I wonder if trying to be the boss
    Has caused the downfall of every man.

I wonder how my country would have been,
    If my ancestors had been a little wiser;
I wonder if I wrote a book,
    Would it change the world, or it wouldn't matter.

I wonder if Martin Luther King would have been born
    If his mother had decided to stay a virgin;
I wonder if he ever would have had a dream,
    If this lad had been born in Belgium.

I wonder if my Daddy would have lived,
    If Adam and Eve had been a little braver;
I wonder if little Chuckie would have been in his grave,
    If I wasn't afraid to ask God for a simple favor.

I wonder how the world would have been,
    If Obama becomes president of America;
I wonder how the whites would feel,
    If their leader's heritage is connected to Africa.

I wonder when women would have voted,
    If they were nothing but simple cowards;
I wonder why Mussolini never opted,
    When they decided to breach this barrier.

    But most of all I wonder;

If God could only rewind the time,
    And oust the day when sin was born;
O Lord, the world would be so fine,
    And never, ever would evil be done.

Oh! How I wonder

Dear Martin Luther King

Dear Martin Luther King,
We blacks are proud of you today
Because of the way you use to think;
We'll remember you every day.

When our fathers and mothers were sold as slaves,
Because they accepted they had inferior minds,
Though now you're in your grave,
You let us know we're one of a kind.

Emancipation proclamation wasn't good enough,
So on the 23rd day of August 1963,
The greatest liberty oration in black history was made;
That today makes us free.

Greater vaults of opportunities are now open,
The banks of injustice has been broken down;
You stood as a hero
And died a great liberator.

You'll forever be remembered,
As long as black men live;
You have won yourself a number
On this great road you have paved.

Though you were assassinated at age 39,
And your greatest dream you dare not see;
I write to inform you that all is fine,
And the world is not what it used to be.

Sincerely yours,
A Black Man

An Old Baptist Church

Above an old Baptist church,
Right off the lane at right,
There an old bird perch
To watch away the night.

In that old Baptist Church,
Daddy became Father-of-the-Year;
Under that very bent arch,
His family will stand in tears.

Beyond an old Baptist Church,
His coffin adorned in bronze lay;
Forever silent below the birch,
Where it is up to this day.

Moods

The referee sounds his whistle,
And the ball goes into the air;
But the entire gym whisper,
That the game isn't fair.

The home team is in red,
And the visitors are in blue;
But the home team looks dead,
And the visitors ain't got a clue.

The mighty Blues takes a lay up,
And the forward goes for the block;
But when he misses, he goes to play off,
And the forward go dance rock.

The ball hits the hoop,
And the air is full with fear;
But the visiting fans gave a whoop,
And the gym is full with tears.

Going To Battle

I hear the war drums beating
As I bid my mama goodbye;
On second thought, I think of quitting,
Cuz I see tears in my mama's eyes.

I heft my bag on my shoulder
And gave my home one final look;
Off I am to across foreign borders,
If I ever come back, I might write myself a book.

I turn around and walk away,
For on these dusty streets I was born and bred;
Mama wants me to stay just one more day.
I'm sorry mama, I just might end up dead.

On the streets, a boy becomes a man,
As childhood memories come flooding back;
I say to myself, "Yes, I can."
For in my heart is where I spark.

I step onto that Tomahawk,
And across the mountains and oceans, we fly;
I don't know if I'll ever come back,
But yet mama pray I wouldn't die.

I hear the missiles landing,
And all around my comrades are dying;
Clutching his heart, my captain is falling,
But I fight on for death itself is nothing.

Boldly, I sprint to catch a falling flag,
And the last thing I think of is my unborn child;
His only memoirs will be daddy's tags,
But life must go on whether I live or die.

Life's Highway

As I stroll down life's highway,
I reminisce on my right and wrong;
If only I had one more chance,
Yet I must remain strong.

I'm sorry for the times I failed,
And for those things I didn't say;
I'm sorry I had to go to jail,
Obnoxious and not knowing the way.

I'm sorry for the times I made you cry,
Being the child you did not know;
I'm sorry you wished that I had died,
Before I ever had the chance to grow.

I'm sorry for the times I walked away,
Because I thought I deserved to leave;
I'm sorry for the times I didn't pray,
And on your knees you prayed and grieved.

I'm sorry for the times you had to watch,
Because your baby wasn't home at three;
I know one day I'll have to crash,
But then, I hope you know I'm free...

Wind

Like my favorite melody,
On a cold, windy night;
I listen to the wind,
And away goes my fright.

Like my favorite blanket,
It wraps itself around me;
It blows away my worries,
And walk me to my dream.

From the gentle, fragrant
Summer wind,
To the wild, scentless
Rainy breeze.

God permits them to blow
On both you, and me;
Whether you like to know
Or not, without a fee.

A True Friend

When the world is closing in,
And you just can't seem to win;
A true friend will always take your hand,
And tell you, "Friend, yes you can."

When your last hope is gone,
And yet you got work undone;
A true friend will always stand by you,
A friend who believes in what you can do.

When your best is not good enough,
And people say you're not worth a hug;
A true friend will always be your guide,
Teach you God's words, and help you abide.

When a secret is too much to bear,
And you're on the verge of sharing tears;
A true friend will always provide a listening ear,
Show you the way and help dissolve your tears.

Daydream

Sometimes when life gets so hard,
I think how much I miss my Dad;
I envision myself with things we had,
And it just makes me pretty mad.

I know one day I will own a yacht,
And I will buy my Mom a diamond ring;
I'm sure my private jet would be the catch,
Then the world will proclaim me a king.

I'll send my kids to school in the Swiss,
I'll build my country beyond her dreams;
God's willing, my kids will be complete wiz,
And every man shall marvel in their fame.

I'll entertain royalties in my home,
And buy a beach all on my own;
For my wife, her grills will be all chrome,
And we'll honeymoon in the Bahamas and Rome.

I'll build a home for orphan kids,
But in my mansion, I'll reminisce;
I'll never teach them how to hate,
And learn in life to never quit.

An African Child's Day

An African child
Wakes up every morning
With tears in his eyes;
He knows what is coming.

Mama has started the household chores,
But the African child is worried;
He has nowhere to go,
If it is school, he better hurry.

There is no pipe borne water,
The well is jammed pack;
If only I can get a liter,
Before the water gets dark.

His uniform is clean, but old,
And that's how far the scholarship goes.
But this little boy, so dauntless and bold,
Pray that one day he stricks gold.

He sits in class absent minded,
He didn't skip breakfast, he just didn't have some.
And yet he thinks, I'm part of God's loving kindness;
The same God that made my mom.

When the school bell rings,
He finally comes off his dream.
In his fantasies, he feels like a king;
But reality hits him with a sting.

In fourteen waking hours,
The African child has only one meal.
Is it breakfast, lunch or dinner, Mr. Myers;
But his pride is as strong as steel.

Recreation is his only source of job,
But how long can he stay;
You don't sell, you don't eat,
A family rule obeyed each day.

Then the sun sets in the west;
And as the full moon rises,
He feels closer to his quest,
But there are still tears in his eyes.

Oh Africa!

Oh Africa, why perish
    when there is so much to live for...
When your resources
    can make you a continent of gold,
When the option to survive
    is your morning coffee,
When your natural parks
    are tourist attraction,
Oh Africa, why perish?

When your generations
    can change the world,
When your politicians
    can reach the global top,
When your rain forest
    can accommodate
Incredible species.

Oh Africa, why perish?

When you are capable of being the best,
    Why be the worst?
When a compromise can be reached,
    Why wage war?
When your history can make us proud,
    Why put us to shame?

Oh Africa, why perish?

Why perish when there's much
    to live for?
When your gallant arm forces

can conquer the world,
When your species
    are one of its kind,
When your scientists are good enough
    to walk the moon,
When your brains can upgrade
    technologies that would overshadow
The predictions of the greatest forecasters?

Oh Africa, why perish?

BEWARE...

Connect with author

Readers of this book are encouraged to contact
Mr. Richards with comments:
E-mail: *riz_b88@hotmail.com*

Connect with Mr. Richards on
Facebook | Twitter | Instagram | LinkedIn

Get updates on upcoming books at:
www.villagetalespublishing.com

All Village Tales Publishing titles, imprints and dis-
tributed lines are available at special quantity discounts
for bulk purchased for sales promotions, premiums,
fundraising, educational or institutional use.

For information, please Visit our website
www.villagetalespublishing.com
email inquiries to
villagetalespub@gmail.com

Other Books by Village Tales Publishing

Available wherever books are sold.
Children's Book

By Ophelia S. Lewis
*I'm About To
Dead Gods HM2
Heart Men (a novel)
Montserrado Stories
Liberia UnScrabbled
*Good Manner Alphabets
My Dear Liberia (Recollections)
Journeys (a Collection of Poems)
*Where in The World Is Liberia
The Dowry of Virgins (and Other Stories)*

By Augustine B. Sherman
War of Morality

By Franck Olivier Houngnikpo
Message To God

By Shedrick B. Seton
The Falcon

By Augustus Y. Voahn
Uncle Jallah Will Fix It

By Roosevelt Richards
Still I Stand

Coming Soon!
*Homeless
Solomon's Porch
Lydia's Dream

Join our mailing list and get updates on new releases, deals, bonus content and other great books from Village Tales Publishing.

Email:
villagetalespub@gmail.com
info@villagetalespublishing.com

Like Us on Facebook
www.facebook.com/villagetalespublishing

www.ingramcontent.com/pod-product-compliance
Lightning Source LLC
Chambersburg PA
CBHW071753020426
42331CB00008B/2304